Self-Portrait as a Sinking Ship

Erica Abbott

TOHO
PUBLISHING

FIRST EDITION

Cover art by Kaitlin O'Donnell
Interior art by Thomas Hale
Original layout and cover design by Tan Nguyen
hyphenatagency.com
Layout by Ana Mitchell

Series editor: Sean Hanrahan

ISBN 978-1-7344992-7-8 (paperback)

"Darkness and Hope" first appeared in *Toho Journal, Vol. 2
No. 1*.

www.tohopub.com

To mom, for believing in me right from the start.

To Dan, this is only the beginning.

CONTENTS

DARKNESS AND HOPE

future me tells
how an entire world
once belonging to the sky
waited on wishes
but darkness is still there
and it threatens to consume
who I am
this you will come to know
things will get better
it may not seem so but
you'll be okay

the me of today
is created from stardust
this heavenly body
holding infinite possibilities
sometimes clear as day
an all-consuming desire to show
who I can never be
when you least expect it
the sun will burn bright
listen to me
you will be okay

DARKNESS

10 THINGS YOU SHOULD KNOW ABOUT MENTAL ILLNESS

1.
I'm fine is the greatest mask you could ever own—
the devil's in one corner, lying undetected, and no
one has ever tried to dance with my demons.
A facade is what makes me acceptable. It keeps
hidden everything that would otherwise scare
if it were to lie in plain sight.

2.
The problem with monsters is they don't wear
name tags when they show up uninvited
to every party you've thrown yourself in the hopes
someone just might notice your breathing shift.
They show up each and every day, shapeshifting,
so I'm none the wiser when they reveal themselves.

3.
In case of emergency, do not break the glass,
for the shards are far too tempting. They glisten
and glint against my skin and, in my mind, I am
already piecing together a tourniquet made
out of regrets. I shattered long ago and failed
to properly fix the cracks lying on the surface.

4.

I am the quietest person you might ever meet
(if you were to give me the chance), but sometimes
the agitation takes over, and I become a violent
storm of emotions instead. You wouldn't
understand, and how could I ever expect you to?
The rains have only ever been kind to you.

5.

Diamonds could be produced out of thin air
with all the pressure I put on myself. If not
from there, then they're bound to appear
when I inevitably erupt. Don't stand too close
because even though I won't mean to hurt you,
I will. You must learn to look past the sparkle.

6.

Most days I could crawl out of my own skin
and beg my body not to return, to forget it.
I am a bag of tangled jitters and nerves
and feel the low tingle and hum of trying
to free myself bubbling at the surface. Leaving
me behind doesn't sound half-bad most days.

7.

Much like the house in *The Wizard of Oz*,
I find myself getting carried away
all while staying right where I am. I am also
the tornado spiraling out of control but keep
myself well-hidden behind a curtain no
person could ever manage to pull back.

8.
When people question what I have to be
so sad about, I don't point because if they
don't see it, then they're bound not to go
looking when I show them what keeps me
up at night—staring at me in the dark.
All I see are vultures circling overhead.

9.
It crashes into me like a wave, knocking me down
and threatening to drown me if I'm not careful.
But I didn't know I was standing in the ocean,
even as it foamed at my feet. The salt no longer
stings the wounds; it just makes them bleed more. I
don't notice the seas redden.

10.
If there were any choice in the matter, would it
matter? You see what you want to see and none
of it is me.
It is not me.
Not from where
I stand.

A YEAR OF DROWNING

It starts with an ending on the surface—
the phone rings from a thousand leagues away,
and the voice on the other end says the fruits
of my labor of the past five years have rotted. I am
silent until I'm not. Until the tiny oceans on my face
do all the talking. Until my breath is all salt and sweat.

Two months later new fruit streams forth, but on the
third day, there is a noticeable absence of light. I find
myself on bereavement leave. But I do not (I cannot)
grieve. My body is far too engulfed for feeling things
like that.

Just when I start to catch my breath, it gets
caught in my throat again. The water rises

      and

      keeps

                             g.

                         n

                    i

              s

          i

    r

//

Fluorescent lights buzz, flicker overhead. From
where I am, the light is bent as it hits the rippling
waters. The doctor speaks, and I listen, but I do
not hear because what he says is far too much for
my waterlogged ears to bear right now. I hold my
breath and hope for the best as I sink further and
further down.

My mother's fine brown hair falls out in clumps,
and I'm tempted to pull my own out in fistfuls
as nails dig into earth no longer in sight. I lay
my head down on the coarse black denim of my
boyfriend's jeans and sleep only to awaken to a
sickness picked up where others are just trying
to get better.

//

I pick at wounds that have scabbed multiple times
over—tell myself it's to save my own skin when it's
really trying to save myself from me. I watch the
blood form tiny pools on my shell. I hope it's only
the bad kind of blood that makes the best escape
artist of them all.

At night, I look at my arms and think how someone
could make a day of playing connect-the-dots
there. Draw the line on how far I'll go. The water
is deep and I'm only a quarter of the way through

it. See how the stars ripple with every movement I dare to make as I fight and flail just to keep from hitting rock bottom?

NOT THE FIRE THAT KILLS ME

It is not the fire that kills
me—it's the smoke
settling in my lungs,
making a home inside
its branches until I suffocate—
a heart squeezed by an invisible
vise. It happens in a blink as
it surrounds me from all sides.
Like a fire,
the smoke inhalation is
slowly killing me.
Except there's no smoke
anywhere in sight—this
is my body being seized
by something invisible

       but just as dangerous.

Like a fire,
I smell fear before
I see it.
Hello, anxiety,
did you bring an extinguisher
this time?

ST. ENDS, PATRON SAINT OF ENDINGS

My best friend and I meet in uniformed shyness at the private school just minutes away from our homes. We never found an arm to place those braided friendship bracelets on, both quiet and coloring outside the lines, only to be told we're doing it wrong. We learn fast to stop trying to straighten each other's paper crowns. Glitter glue, never quite dry, manages to hold us together for eight years until we go off to different schools and never speak again, save for all the conversations I wish we would have had before our shared school of limits was tested.

We walk into different rooms where the only people who know our names are those with an attendance sheet. I wish those bracelets never would have snapped under the pressure we put on them. I spend an entire year sitting at a table in the cafeteria filled with girls who never speak one word to me. I never say a single syllable to them either. At night, once-sentimental collages turn into confetti at my feet.

Yesterday, I found the other half of a plastic "Best Friends" heart necklace, the one with the broken

silver chain, that we gifted to each other all those
years ago—the side I kept reads: *st*
                              ends

And I think how very fitting it is to be the patron
saint of endings.

Why can't I just pick up the phone, say hello—
how have you been?

FEVER PITCH

I write at a fever pitch to starve the fever dreams
      trying to feed on my mind, whether I'm
      asleep or awake.
Try to keep them at bay, but they stay
      they stay
      they stay
      they stay.
No matter how many times I've tried
      to chase them away, they return,
      each one stronger than before—
      tearing at the seams.
These fingers can barely keep up
      as my mind races on and against the hands of time—
      these pages become bloodied.
Can these chapters ever hold the pain
      that has long been kept inside?
      Making a home in my nightmares—
      this body's a simple pawn.

I write . . .
             But will it ever be enough?
             Will it ever be?
             Will it ever?
             Will I?

SANDCASTLES AND THE SEA

Where once you held me
     like sand in your hands,
          building castles as you built me up,

          I now slip through your fingers
     like water—destroying everything in our path.
And isn't it poetic?

How the things meant to protect us
     can so easily crumble—break, fall
          like a once-mighty empire.

          Did we build too close to the sea,
     letting the tides wash us away?
Or were our walls just too high,

too resentful, too unconquerable?
     I tried to save what was left
          while all you did was try to knock it down.

          I try to blink the saltwater away—
     make my eyes flutter like that of a seabird
in flight—make no mistake

I try   and   I try   and   I try
        but they fall onto trembling hands
                        that once steadied your hurricanes.

                        I don't fear you, never once did—
            this vulnerability, however, makes me
fear wearing my emotions like a lighthouse

glowing ever-so-brightly even in the dark.
        Maybe they should be kept hidden,
                but I know that's impossible.

                I feel to the depths of an oceanic trench.
        And eventually these teardrops will e v a p o r a t e
unless they find their way to a page,

where their stains will forever be
        a permanent reminder anchored to words
                that were only ever meant

                for you.

        Now they are (and only ever should have been)

all mine.

ENDING BY BEGINNING

When we emerge from this, we will be better, breathe new life into the day, open our eyes toward the sun.

When we emerge from this, this will all feel like a nightmare, like all we ever needed was a pinch to wake us.

When we emerge from this, we will walk into the eye of the storm, not caring whether it started as calm or not.

When we emerge from this, this will all become a bad memory, repressed by those who don't have the strength to remember.

When we emerge from this, we will run to each other, swear we won't let this happen again, not again.

When we emerge from this, this will be both an ending and a beginning.

When we emerge from this—will we emerge from this?

SELF-PORTRAIT AS A SINKING SHIP

1.
Mayday. Mayday. Mayday.
Every last action was exhausted
long ago. No one was listening
except for when to jump ship
before the water even hit their feet.

2.
A vessel. Its empty shell—
all a form for shallow
revelries that no one
will remember tomorrow.
But everyone will be lining up
to dive deep and explore once
it has hit rock bottom.

3.
My center of gravity has
always been low. Just a disaster
waiting to happen.
(There's never been any
lifeboats aboard).

4.
While everyone's safe on land,
I'm still taking on water. Everyone
still counts their blessings
they escaped when they could.
Beacons signal in the distance.
There are not enough words
in the world to capture how
it radiates.

5.
No distress signals were ever responded to.
But somehow, against all odds,
I am still staying afloat.

HOPE

DAYS LIKE TODAY

On days like today, I think I'd like
To be a bird that can escape
Whenever they choose (as long as
Their wings aren't broken).

                    Here lies the problem.

On days like today, I am more
Question mark than woman.
My shoulders hang stiff over my ears—
This body twists into something
Unrecognizable just trying to live.
It forgot its song long ago.

                    Never did it sound so pretty.

On days like today, the walls aren't
Just closing in, they're crumbling.
My foundation could once withstand
The strongest earthquakes but these days
Aftershocks have the whole house shaking.

                    My body's no longer a shelter.

On days like today, I think only
Of the future—every word still

To say, each heartbeat left to come.
You and me—
Because it's all that's keeping me alive.

That has to be enough for now.

SIXTY PERCENT WATER

Your isolation is not a boat
struggling to stay afloat
in the merciless, stormy summer seas;
you just need to trust in your strength
and work hard to keep this vessel
above the rogue waves.

Your tears are not the unrelenting floods
and hurricanes eroding the shores or coastlines;
you are free to move on from the things that seek
to turn you into a kind of disappearing act.

Your pain is not a tsunami swallowing
an entire city with its angry waters
in mere seconds; you are the fight left behind
in its wake—and you will face those battles
every single day.

Your fears are not cyclones spiraling
wildly out of control, destroying everything
in their path; you just live unapologetically,
no matter how others threaten to use
those fears against you.

You will not run dry as droughts ravage
the earth, causing fissures

to run deep and long; keep going
because all you need is inside of you—
let it flow through you and into the soil.

You are not unforgiving disasters,
wreaking irrevocable damage.
You are a life-sustaining force,
and you will rebuild yourself. You
hold more than enough power
to make it happen.

SAVING GRACE

I was lost in the dark for so long,
I feared the light would never again find me.
Questioned why it would ever seek me out
when an unending night is all my eyes could see.

I hoped to use the stars as my guide,
but as it turns out, even they don't stick around.
My story could be written only by me,
and in slow dancing with death, hope was found.

I had to free myself
          from the rhymes
          the lines
clawing to get out of my head.
So I picked up my pen
          let it speak
          watched it bleed.
But most importantly
I chose to

          Stay
                    Stay
                              Stay
                                        Stay

and you will, too.

You may look for a million reasons to go,
but the Earth needs you here for no one
can tell a story quite like the person who lived it.

So pick up your pen and
        let the ink be the only thing
        that spills across these pages—
        there are many chapters left to write.

And may these words be a light
when all is seemingly lost
in the dark.

LIGHT IN THE FOG

I've always loved the way the light
        interacts with fog—
the way it filters through like
        moonlight on a cobweb.

The fog rolls across the land
        as the blue spirits dance
upon the green heavens of
        the earth.

And the concave light breaks
        through the silhouetted trees—
forming ripples, turning smoke
        into an iridescent kaleidoscope.

While the sunlight rises
        over the clouded horizon
the fog settles over
        fresh drops of dew.

Light passes through the droplets—
        creating a prismatic effect
and the transparent shadows of morning
        continue to brighten the fog.

As these events unfold
        we lie in silence

in this moment—
        you'll be the fog
        and I'll be the light.

HOME

I close my eyes, and I'm there,
standing tall among buildings meant
to make me feel small—rising
from the depths of an underground
just as busy.

Call this hell,
but to me it's an all-embracing landscape
begging for skyward attention.

I emerge from one crowd
to a sea of thousands
(the only sea I've ever needed).
Each wave of people and machine
finding exactly where they need to be
along the maze-like shores.
The ripples are yellow—screaming
out their own distinct bawls.
A language of honking horns
and screeching brakes.

Music born from makeshift instruments
carved into skin is played with a particular
passion understood by many and pours
into the streets from sidewalk grates.

Dreams have been discovered here. They've died here. Most of all though, they have come alive here, under a canopy of invisible stars.

Energies can be felt in the air,
and it holds me to this Earth
better than gravity ever could.
But, oh, how none of this is the same
without you right here by my side—
lost everywhere but in your arms.

How I long to be back there—home.
So I take a deep breath,
close my eyes,
and I'm there.

STORIES ON OUR SKIN

When I look at people
I can't help
but see stories
etched delicately
across their faces.

Sometimes they are hidden
in hand lines and wrinkles;
beneath eyes and fingerprints.

They are told
through markings on their body:
every stretch mark, blemish,
bruise, and scar.

Within the pages of their skin
are epics, sonnets, and truths.
Love notes and haikus and tales
from a wild youth.

They live these stories out boldly.
Setting themselves apart in italic type—
freckles like ellipses,
smiles a simile,
lips curve into parentheses
(while eyes beg for answers).

Words pour from their hearts
as letters are shaken from their hair.
Their bodies are the greatest book
someone will ever read—
the kind you can't put down
(no matter how hard you try).

So when their story is at last freed,
they will be held together by only
a cracked spine—and while my chapters
are far from over, I wonder:
when people look at me
what kind of story
do I tell?

A THOUSAND TIMES

You are my calm amid the chaos.
I lay my head on your chest
and the rest of the world softens.

A thousand times I've said your name
and a thousand times it's sounded
something like a prayer meant to be
recited time and time again
until we both believe in the
miracles living inside both of us.
I fold my hands, bend my knees
to the floor; thank the universe
              over and
                      over
and over time my words will become
less of a battle cry and more of a way
to set us both free.

It won't always be like this.
It can't.
It cannot.

A thousand times will we look back—
though never with regret—at just how
far we've come and the future that
lies ahead.

You will never be the rainbow
that follows a storm—for you
endure the storm right by my side.
The rain.
The wind.
The thunder.
None of it can touch me when your body
becomes a shelter and I take cover.

You are my calm;
my love
my life—
but most importantly—
you will always be the one
who, from our beginning,
saved me.

THE MAGIC OF BECOMING

throw caution to the wind / be reckless / but never
/ with your heart / open up your hand / let the air
/ spin stories / in your palm / pluck music notes /
from all your / favorite songs / call it an anthem /
play it time / and time again / when life becomes
/ far too heavy / tie a balloon / to your wrist and /
let it keep you / grounded / plant your feet firmly
/ in the earth but / never so permanently your /
roots forget how to move / place / to place / your
fingers across / your ribcage and feel / how an
entire world / beats inside you / whispering / you
are free / to live / live / be alive / you are breathing
/ becoming / magic with every / exhale

HOW TO STARGAZE THROUGH THE LIGHT POLLUTION

1.
Download that star finder app.
Turn on the augmented reality feature
and hold your phone up to the sky.
Watch as constellations you know
have always been there (but have
never truly seen) appear right before
your eyes.

2.
Rub your eyes—hard.
Until phosphenes overtake
your vision. Let the colorful
shapes transfer you to another
world just beyond your line of sight.

3.
Stick dozens of phosphorescent
star stickers onto the ceiling of your bedroom.
Look on as the glow-in-the-dark decals
lull you softly to sleep.

4.
Turn off every single light in this city. No—
to hell with that—make it the world. Cut

the problem off at its source. Billions of people
will open their eyes, emerge from their homes,
climb up to their roof and cry as the cosmos
opens up before them.

5.
Gaze into the eyes
of your lover. Lose yourself
in every shooting star and supernova
lighting up their face. This is how
you rediscover the universe.

ACKNOWLEDGEMENTS

Thank you to *Toho Publishing* and especially Andrés Cruciani and Sean Hanrahan for taking such good care of my words and supporting me wholeheartedly. To the incredible poets I've gotten to work with as part of this publishing series: Israel Colón, Elisha Gibson, Jonathan Koven, Neti Neti, Ashley Rivera, and Leena Taylor. It was an honor to go on this journey with every single one of you.

To all the teachers/mentors I've had over the years: John Brown and Drew Cocco—you were some of the best teachers I never had. I'm grateful for everything I learned from you in high school poetry club and literary magazine. Heather Minauro, thank you for being one of the first to help foster my words. Sierra DeMulder, your WORDY workshop forever changed me as a writer. Megan Falley, Melissa Sussens, and the entire Poems That Don't Suck class, you make me a better poet each and every day.

To everyone in the poetry community that I've come to know and be inspired by: Amy Kay, William Bortz, Renee DeCoskey, Kari Ann Ebert, Courtney LeBlanc, and so many more. To the artists who provided the cover art and interior images for this chapbook: Kait O'Donnell and Thomas Hale, your creativity knows no bounds.

To my friends and family. Especially Mom and Dad—I'm so thankful for your unending support. Dan, your light and love has and will always be a source of hope for me. This is truly just the beginning. I love you all. Thank you for believing in me.

ABOUT THE POET

Erica Abbott is a Philadelphia-based poet and writer. She has been writing for over fifteen years, and her work has appeared in *Toho Journal*, *perhappened*, *Flora Fiction*, and other journals. *Self-Portrait as a Sinking Ship* is her first chapbook. Follow her on Instagram at @poetry_erica and on Twitter at @erica_abbott.